MASTERING MONEY MINDSET: A YOUNG ADULT'S GUIDE TO FRUGAL LIVING AND SMART INVESTING

K SHAIL

Contents

Preface

Welcome to the world of financial empowerment! As you hold this book in your hands, you're embarking on a journey that has the potential to transform your relationship with money and unlock new possibilities for your financial future. Whether you're a recent graduate entering the workforce, a young professional navigating the complexities of early adulthood, or simply someone seeking to gain a better understanding of personal finance, this book is designed to meet you where you are and guide you towards greater financial success and fulfillment.

The inspiration for this book stems from a simple yet profound realization: that financial literacy is not just a skill, but a fundamental pillar of personal empowerment. In today's fast-paced and ever-changing world, the ability to manage money wisely and make informed financial decisions is essential for achieving both short-term stability and long-term prosperity. Yet, for many young adults, the world of personal finance can seem overwhelming, confusing, or even intimidating.

That's where this book comes in. My goal is to demystify the world of finance and make it accessible to readers of all backgrounds and experience levels. Whether you're a total novice or someone with some prior knowledge of finance, you'll find valuable insights, practical tips, and actionable strategies that you can apply to your own financial journey.

Throughout these pages, we'll cover a wide range of topics, from the basics of budgeting and saving to the nuances of investment strategies and retirement planning. We'll explore the psychology of money, the importance of mindfulness in financial decision-making, and the role of resilience in overcoming financial challenges. We'll also delve into practical advice for managing debt, building credit, and navigating economic uncertainties.

But more than just providing information, this book is about empowerment. It's about giving you the knowledge, tools, and confidence you need to take control of your financial destiny and create a life of abundance and fulfillment. Whether your goal is to buy a home, start a business, travel the world, or simply achieve financial peace of mind, the principles and strategies outlined in this book can help you get there.

As you read through these pages, I encourage you to approach each chapter with an open mind and a willingness to learn. Take notes, ask questions, and reflect on how the concepts and strategies discussed can be applied to your own life. And remember, financial empowerment is not just about mastering numbers and formulas—it's about aligning your money with your values, goals, and aspirations, and using it as a tool to create the life you desire.

I want to extend my heartfelt gratitude to you, the reader, for embarking on this journey with me. It's my sincere hope that this book serves as a valuable resource and a source of inspiration as you navigate your own path towards financial success and fulfillment. Together, let's empower ourselves to achieve our dreams and create a brighter future for ourselves and our loved ones.

K Shail

CHAPTER ONE

Introduction: Unlocking the Power of Your Money Mindset

Money holds a significant place in our lives. It dictates where we live, what we eat, how we spend our time, and even our level of freedom. Yet, despite its pervasive influence, many of us fail to recognize the profound impact that our mindset towards money has on our financial well-being. In this introductory chapter, we embark on a journey to uncover the transformative power of our money mindset. We'll explore how our beliefs, attitudes, and perceptions about money shape our financial decisions, behaviors, and ultimately, our financial outcomes. By gaining insight into our money mindset, we can take control of our financial destiny, make more informed choices, and pave the way towards greater financial success and fulfillment.

Understanding Your Money Mindset

Our money mindset is the lens through which we view and interact with money. It encompasses our beliefs, attitudes, and emotions towards money and financial matters. Our money mindset is shaped by a variety of factors including our upbringing, cultural influences, past experiences and societal norms.

For example, if we were raised in a household where money was scarce and financial struggle was a constant, we may develop a scarcity mindset. This mindset may lead us to believe that money is hard to come by and that we must hoard it and avoid spending it at all costs.

Conversely, if we were raised in an environment of abundance where money was viewed as a tool for growth and opportunity, we may develop an abundance mindset. This mindset may lead us to believe that money is abundant and that there are always opportunities to create wealth and achieve financial success.

The Power of Beliefs and Attitudes

Our beliefs and attitudes towards money play a crucial role in shaping our financial behaviors and outcomes. If we believe that money is scarce and that there will never be enough, we may adopt a scarcity mindset that leads us to engage in behaviors such as living paycheck to paycheck, hoarding money, and avoiding investing. Conversely, if we believe that money is abundant and that opportunities for wealth creation are all around us, we may adopt an abundance mindset that leads us to take proactive steps to grow our wealth and achieve financial success.

For example, someone with a scarcity mindset may feel anxious and stressed about money, constantly worrying about how they will pay their bills and make ends meet. This anxiety may lead them to make impulsive financial decisions and engage in behaviors such as overspending and taking on high-interest debt. On the other hand, someone with an abundance mindset may feel confident and optimistic about their financial future, believing that they have the ability to create wealth and achieve their financial goals. This confidence may lead them to make strategic financial decisions and take calculated risks in pursuit of their goals.

The Influence of Past Experiences

Our past experiences with money also play a significant role in shaping our money mindset. Positive experiences, such as receiving praise for saving money or achieving financial goals, can reinforce positive financial behaviors and attitudes. Conversely, negative experiences, such as struggling with debt or experiencing financial hardship, can create limiting beliefs and attitudes that hinder our financial success.

Someone who grew up in a household where money was a constant source of stress and conflict may develop a negative association with money and view it as something to be feared and avoided. This negative association may lead them to engage in behaviors such as overspending and impulse buying in an attempt to alleviate their stress and anxiety. On the other hand, someone who grew up in a household where money was managed responsibly and financial goals were prioritized may develop a positive association with money and view it as a tool for achieving their dreams and aspirations. This positive association may lead them to engage in behaviors such as saving and investing in pursuit of their goals.

Cultural and Societal Influences

In addition to the influences of the past, our cultural and societal influences also play a significant role in shaping our money mindset. Cultural norms, values, and expectations surrounding money can vary widely depending on factors such as ethnicity, socioeconomic status, and geographic location.

In some cultures there may be a strong emphasis on saving money and living frugally, while in others, there may be pressure to spend money on status symbols and material possessions. Similarly, societal pressures and expectations can influence our money mindset, leading us to engage in behaviors such as keeping up with the Joneses and spending beyond our means in an attempt to fit in and maintain a certain lifestyle.

The Importance of Self-Awareness

Self-awareness thus becomes the cornerstone of unlocking the power of our money mindset. We might belong to any culture or we may be harbouring any pre-conceived mind-set, but by becoming aware of our beliefs, attitudes, and emotions towards money, we can begin to identify patterns and behaviors that may be holding us back from achieving our financial goals.

For example, if we notice that we have a tendency to overspend when we're feeling stressed or anxious, we can take steps to address the underlying emotions driving this behavior, such as practicing stress management techniques or seeking support from a financial coach. Similarly, if we notice that we have a negative association with money due to past experiences, if we can identify our own mindset and what it might have been influenced by, we can work on reframing our beliefs and attitudes into an abundant mindset to create a more positive relationship with money.

Learnings

In conclusion, our money mindset is a powerful force that shapes our financial behaviors, habits, and outcomes. By gaining insight into our beliefs, attitudes, and perceptions towards money, we can take control of our financial destiny, make more informed choices, and pave the way towards greater financial success and fulfillment. Throughout this book, we will explore strategies for transforming our money mindset, overcoming limiting beliefs and attitudes, and cultivating a mindset of abundance and empowerment. By unlocking the power of our money mindset, we can create a brighter financial future for ourselves and generations to come.

CHAPTER TWO

Understanding Your Relationship with Money

Money is a powerful force in our lives, shaping our choices, influencing our opportunities, and impacting our overall well-being. Yet, our relationship with money is often complex and multifaceted, influenced by a variety of factors ranging from upbringing and culture to personal experiences and societal norms. In this chapter, we will delve into the intricacies of our relationship with money, exploring its origins, dynamics, and implications for our financial health and happiness.

The Influence of Upbringing

Our relationship with money often begins in childhood, shaped by the attitudes, beliefs, and behaviors modeled by our parents or caregivers. Whether we grew up in a household of abundance or scarcity, our early experiences with money leave a lasting imprint on our financial mindset and behaviors.

Children raised in an environment where money was managed wisely and financial responsibility was emphasized are likely to develop healthy money habits and attitudes towards saving and investing. Conversely, children raised in a household where money was a source of stress or conflict may develop negative associations with money and struggle with financial management later in life.

Money as a Source of Emotion

Money is often intertwined with our emotions, evoking feelings of security, anxiety, or even guilt. Our financial decisions are frequently driven by emotional factors rather than rational considerations, leading to behaviors such as impulse buying, overspending, or avoiding financial planning altogether.

Fear of scarcity or loss may drive individuals to hoard money or avoid taking financial risks, even when it may be beneficial in the long run. Similarly, feelings of inadequacy or comparison may lead to overspending in an attempt to keep up with others or maintain a certain lifestyle.

The Impact of Life Experiences

Life experiences, both positive and negative, can significantly impact our relationship with money. Windfall inheritances, job losses, or unexpected expenses can all shape our attitudes and behaviors towards money, influencing our financial decisions and priorities.

Experiencing financial hardship or bankruptcy may lead to feelings of shame or inadequacy, impacting self-esteem and confidence in managing money. Conversely, achieving financial success or receiving a significant windfall may boost feelings of security and empowerment, motivating individuals to take more risks or pursue long-term financial goals.

Reflection and Self-Awareness

Understanding our relationship with money requires reflection and self-awareness. It involves examining our beliefs, attitudes, and behaviors surrounding money with honesty and curiosity.

For instance, individuals may reflect on questions such as: What messages did I receive about money growing up? How do I feel about my current financial situation? What are my long-term financial goals and aspirations?

By engaging in this process of self-reflection, we gain valuable insights into our relationship with money and the patterns that shape our financial behaviors. Armed with this awareness, we can begin to challenge limiting beliefs, cultivate healthier financial habits, and ultimately, achieve greater financial well-being and fulfillment.

Cultivating a Healthy Relationship with Money

Building a healthy relationship with money requires intentional effort and ongoing self-reflection. It involves developing an understanding of our values, priorities, and goals, and aligning our financial decisions with these principles.

Individuals should set aside time to create a budget, track their spending, and identify areas where they can save or invest more effectively. They should also seek out resources and support, such as financial education courses or professional advice, to help them navigate complex financial decisions and achieve their goals.

In addition, cultivating gratitude and mindfulness can help individuals develop a more positive outlook on their financial situation and appreciate the abundance in their lives. By focusing on what they have rather than what they lack, individuals can foster a sense of contentment and satisfaction with their financial circumstances, regardless of their income or material possessions.

Learnings

Our relationship with money is a reflection of our values, beliefs, and experiences. By understanding the influences that shape our financial mindset and behaviors, we can take proactive steps to cultivate a healthier relationship with money and achieve greater financial well-being and fulfillment.

In this chapter, we explored the impact of emotions and life experiences on our relationship with money. We discussed the importance of self-reflection and self-awareness in understanding our financial mindset and identified strategies for cultivating a healthy relationship with money.

As we continue our journey towards financial empowerment and success, it's essential to recognize that our relationship with money is dynamic and evolving. By embracing curiosity, self-awareness, and a growth mindset, we can navigate the complexities of personal finance with confidence and achieve our financial goals with clarity and purpose.

CHAPTER THREE

The Psychology of Frugality: How Your Brain Works

Frugality, often associated with careful budgeting and prudent spending, is more than just a financial strategy—it's a mindset deeply rooted in psychology. In this chapter, we'll explore the intricate workings of the brain and how they influence our attitudes and behaviors towards money and consumption. Understanding the psychology of frugality can empower us to make more intentional financial decisions, prioritize long-term goals, and ultimately achieve greater financial well-being.

The Brain's Reward System

At the core of the psychology of frugality lies the brain's reward system. This system is responsible for processing pleasure and reinforcement, guiding our behaviors towards actions perceived as rewarding. When we engage in frugal behaviors, such as saving money or avoiding unnecessary expenses, the brain's reward system is activated, releasing neurotransmitters like dopamine and serotonin.

Research has shown that the brain's reward system responds not only to external rewards like money and possessions but also to internal rewards such as pride, accomplishment, and self-control. Frugal behaviors, such as sticking to a budget or resisting impulse purchases, can trigger a sense of satisfaction and pride, activating the brain's reward system and reinforcing these behaviors.

Understanding how the brain's reward system responds to frugality sheds light on why some individuals find satisfaction and fulfillment in saving money, while others struggle to resist the temptation of instant gratification. By tapping into the reward system's potential, we can train our brains to associate frugal behaviors with feelings of pleasure and accomplishment, making it easier to maintain disciplined financial habits.

Habit Formation and Conditioning

The brain is wired to seek efficiency and conserve energy, leading to the formation of habits and routines. Frugality, like any other behavior, can become ingrained through repeated practice and conditioning. When we consistently make mindful choices to save money or avoid unnecessary expenses, we reinforce neural pathways associated with frugal behavior.

Over time, these habits become automatic, requiring less cognitive effort and decision-making. By establishing frugal habits such as meal planning, comparison shopping, and prioritizing needs over wants, we can create a lifestyle that supports our financial goals and values.

Cognitive Biases and Frugal Living

Cognitive biases are systematic patterns of deviation from rationality in judgment, often influencing our perceptions and decisions related to frugality. For example, the scarcity bias, which states that the more difficult it is to acquire an item the more we value it, may lead us to hoard resources or avoid spending money, even when it's in our best interest to do so. Similarly, the endowment effect, which is a cognitive bias that causes people to value something they own more than something that don't, may cause us to overvalue possessions we already own, making it difficult to part with them even if they no longer serve us.

By recognizing these cognitive biases and their impact on our financial decisions, we can mitigate their effects and make more rational choices with our money. Strategies such as reframing and decision-making tools like cost-benefit analysis can help counteract the influence of cognitive biases on frugal living.

Emotional Responses to Frugality

Frugality is not solely a rational endeavor—it's also deeply intertwined with our emotions and sense of identity. For some, practicing frugality may evoke feelings of pride, self-discipline, and accomplishment. For others, it may trigger feelings of deprivation, shame, or anxiety.

Understanding the emotional aspect of frugality is essential for maintaining a healthy relationship with money. By reframing frugality as a positive choice that aligns with our values and goals, we can cultivate a sense of empowerment and satisfaction in our financial decisions. Strategies such as mindfulness and self-compassion can help navigate the emotional challenges of frugality, allowing us to embrace it as a path to greater financial freedom and fulfillment.

Overcoming Psychological Barriers to Frugality

Despite its benefits, embracing frugality can be challenging due to various psychological barriers. Fear of missing out (FOMO), social pressure, and instant gratification are just a few of the factors that may hinder our ability to adopt a frugal lifestyle.

However, by leveraging strategies such as goal-setting, visualization, and accountability, we can overcome these barriers and cultivate a mindset of abundance and resourcefulness. By reframing frugality as a conscious choice that aligns with our values and aspirations, we can unlock its full potential to enhance our financial well-being and quality of life.

Learnings

The psychology of frugality offers valuable insights into the inner workings of the brain and its influence on our financial behaviors. By understanding the brain's reward system, habit formation, cognitive biases, and emotional responses, we can navigate the complexities of frugal living with greater awareness and intentionality.

By overcoming psychological barriers and embracing frugality as a path to financial freedom and fulfillment, we pave the way for greater financial well-being and peace of mind. Through self-awareness, mindfulness, and strategic interventions, we can harness the power of our brains to achieve our long-term financial goals and lead more meaningful lives. Ultimately, the psychology of frugality empowers us to take control of our finances, prioritize what truly matters, and create a brighter future for ourselves and generations to come.

CHAPTER FOUR

Overcoming Financial FOMO: Embracing Frugality in a Consumerist World

In a world driven by consumerism and the constant bombardment of advertisements and social media influencers promoting the latest products and trends, it's easy to fall prey to Financial FOMO (Fear of Missing Out). Financial FOMO refers to the anxiety and pressure individuals feel when they perceive others enjoying material possessions or experiences that they cannot afford. This chapter delves into the challenges posed by Financial FOMO and offers strategies for embracing frugality and finding contentment amidst a consumerist culture.

Understanding Financial FOMO

Financial FOMO stems from a combination of social comparison and the desire for social acceptance and validation. In today's hyperconnected world, social media platforms showcase curated versions of people's lives, often highlighting material possessions and experiences that may evoke envy or feelings of inadequacy in others. The fear of missing out on these experiences can drive individuals to overspend, accumulate debt, or prioritize short-term gratification over long-term financial security.

The Impact of Financial FOMO

Financial FOMO can have detrimental effects on individuals' financial health and well-being. It can lead to impulsive spending, excessive debt, and a lack of savings, ultimately hindering individuals from achieving their long-term financial goals. Moreover, constantly comparing oneself to others and feeling inadequate can take a toll on mental health, contributing to stress, anxiety, and low self-esteem.

Strategies for Overcoming Financial FOMO

1. *Practice Gratitude and Contentment*: Cultivating gratitude and contentment can help counteract the feelings of envy and inadequacy that fuel Financial FOMO. By focusing on what we already have and appreciating life's simple pleasures, we can shift our perspective away from material possessions and towards experiences and relationships that bring true fulfillment.

2. *Set Clear Financial Goals*: Setting clear financial goals based on our values and priorities can provide a sense of purpose and direction, helping us resist the urge to compare ourselves to others. By defining our own definition of success and progress, we can measure our financial well-being based on our own standards rather than external benchmarks.

3. *Practice Mindful Spending*: Mindful spending involves being intentional and conscious about how we allocate our financial resources. Before making a purchase, ask yourself whether it aligns with your values and priorities and whether it will bring lasting satisfaction. Avoid making impulse purchases or succumbing to the pressure of fleeting trends.

4. *Limit Exposure to Triggers*: Recognize the triggers that exacerbate Financial FOMO, such as excessive time spent on social media or exposure to advertising. Limiting your exposure to these triggers can help reduce feelings of envy and inadequacy, allowing you to focus on your own financial journey without comparison.

5. *Practice Delayed Gratification*: Embracing delayed gratification involves postponing immediate desires in favor of long-term rewards. Instead of succumbing to the impulse to make a purchase or indulge in a luxury experience, practice patience and discipline by saving towards meaningful goals that align with your values and aspirations.

6. *Build a Supportive Community*: Surround yourself with like-minded individuals who share your values and support your financial goals. Whether it's joining a frugal living group, participating in online forums,

or attending financial education workshops, building a supportive community can provide encouragement, accountability, and inspiration on your journey towards frugality.

7. *Focus on Financial Education*: Knowledge is power when it comes to overcoming Financial FOMO. Invest in financial education and literacy to gain a better understanding of personal finance concepts, budgeting strategies, and investment options. By empowering yourself with knowledge, you can make informed financial decisions that align with your goals and values.

8. *Practice Self-Compassion*: Be kind to yourself and recognize that everyone's financial journey is unique. Instead of comparing yourself to others or berating yourself for past financial mistakes, practice self-compassion and forgiveness. Celebrate your progress, no matter how small, and focus on the positive steps you're taking towards financial well-being.

Embracing Frugality in a Consumerist World

Frugality is not about deprivation or sacrifice—it's about intentional living and prioritizing what truly matters. By embracing frugality, individuals can cultivate a sense of empowerment, freedom, and contentment amidst a consumerist culture. Frugality encourages resourcefulness, creativity, and mindful consumption, allowing individuals to live more sustainably and responsibly while achieving their financial goals.

Learnings

Financial FOMO can be a powerful force, driving individuals to overspend, accumulate debt, and prioritize short-term gratification over long-term financial security. However, by understanding the underlying causes of Financial FOMO and implementing strategies to overcome it, individuals can reclaim control of their finances and find contentment amidst a consumerist world.

By practicing gratitude, setting clear financial goals, and adopting mindful spending habits, individuals can cultivate a sense of empowerment and fulfillment that transcends material possessions. Through self-awareness, education, and support from like-minded communities,

individuals can overcome Financial FOMO and achieve greater financial
well-being and peace of mind.

CHAPTER FIVE

Budgeting Basics: Taking Control of Your Finances

Budgeting is the cornerstone of financial success. It provides a roadmap for managing income, expenses, and savings, enabling individuals to take control of their finances and work towards their financial goals. In this chapter, we will explore the fundamentals of budgeting, from creating a budget to tracking expenses and adjusting financial priorities. By mastering budgeting basics, individuals can build a solid foundation for achieving financial stability, security, and freedom.

Understanding the Purpose of Budgeting

At its core, budgeting is about aligning income with expenses and savings goals. It serves as a tool for tracking financial inflows and outflows, identifying areas of overspending or waste, and making informed decisions about resource allocation. By creating a budget, individuals can prioritize their financial goals, whether it's paying off debt, saving for a major purchase, or investing for the future.

Creating a Budget

The first step in budgeting is to gather information about your income, expenses, and financial goals. Start by listing all sources of income, including salaries, wages, bonuses, and investment returns. Next, categorize your expenses into fixed expenses (e.g., rent, mortgage, utilities) and variable expenses (e.g., groceries, entertainment, dining out).

Once you have a clear picture of your income and expenses, allocate funds towards savings and debt repayment goals. Set aside a portion of your income for emergency savings, retirement contributions, and debt payments, prioritizing high-interest debt first.

Tracking Expenses

Tracking expenses is essential for staying within budget and identifying areas for improvement. Use a spreadsheet, budgeting app, or financial tracking tool to record all expenses, including cash transactions and credit card purchases. Be diligent about categorizing expenses and reviewing spending patterns regularly.

Consider using the envelope method or cash-only system for discretionary spending categories to prevent overspending. Allocate a set amount of cash for categories like groceries, dining out, and entertainment each month and only spend what's available in each envelope.

Adjusting Financial Priorities

As life circumstances change, so too may financial priorities. Periodically review your budget and adjust allocations based on changes in income, expenses, or financial goals. For example, if you receive a salary increase or bonus, consider allocating a portion towards savings or investments to accelerate progress towards your goals.

Similarly, if you encounter unexpected expenses or financial setbacks, be prepared to reassess your budget and make necessary adjustments. Look for opportunities to reduce discretionary spending or find creative solutions to lower fixed expenses, such as refinancing loans or negotiating bills.

Budgeting Strategies

Several budgeting strategies can help individuals manage their finances effectively and achieve their goals:

1. *Zero-Based Budgeting*: In zero-based budgeting, every dollar of income is allocated towards specific expenses or savings goals, leaving no money unaccounted for. This approach encourages individuals to prioritize spending and ensure that every dollar serves a purpose.
2. *50/30/20 Rule*: The 50/30/20 rule allocates 50% of income towards needs (e.g., housing, utilities), 30% towards wants (e.g., entertainment,

dining out), and 20% towards savings and debt repayment. This rule provides a simple framework for balancing spending and savings priorities.

3. ***Envelope Budgeting***: Envelope budgeting involves allocating cash into envelopes for different spending categories and only spending what's available in each envelope. This method helps individuals control discretionary spending and avoid overspending in specific categories.

4. ***Pay Yourself First***: Paying yourself first involves prioritizing savings by setting aside a portion of income towards savings goals before allocating funds towards other expenses. This approach ensures that saving becomes a priority and helps individuals build a financial safety net over time.

5. ***Automated Savings***: Automating savings contributions can help individuals stay consistent with their savings goals and avoid the temptation to spend money earmarked for savings. Set up automatic transfers from your checking account to designated savings or investment accounts each month to ensure consistent progress towards your goals.

The Benefits of Budgeting

Budgeting offers numerous benefits beyond just managing finances:

1. ***Financial Awareness***: Budgeting promotes financial awareness by providing insights into income, expenses, and spending habits. By tracking expenses and reviewing spending patterns regularly, individuals can identify areas for improvement and make informed decisions about resource allocation.

2. ***Goal Achievement***: Budgeting helps individuals prioritize financial goals and allocate funds towards savings, debt repayment, and investments. By setting clear goals and tracking progress, individuals can stay motivated and focused on achieving their objectives.

3. ***Financial Security***: Budgeting provides a framework for building financial security and stability. By establishing emergency savings, paying off debt, and saving for the future, individuals can protect themselves against unexpected expenses and financial setbacks.

4. ***Reduced Stress***: Financial uncertainty and anxiety are common sources of stress for many individuals. Budgeting can help alleviate stress by providing a sense of control and empowerment over one's financial situation. By having a clear plan in place, individuals can feel more confident and secure about their financial future.

Learnings

Budgeting is a fundamental tool for managing finances, achieving financial goals, and building a secure financial future. By understanding the purpose of budgeting, creating a budget, tracking expenses, and adjusting financial priorities as needed, individuals can take control of their finances and work towards their goals with confidence.

By implementing budgeting strategies such as zero-based budgeting, the 50/30/20 rule, envelope budgeting, paying yourself first, and automated savings, individuals can maximize the benefits of budgeting and optimize their financial well-being. Ultimately, budgeting empowers individuals to make informed decisions about money, prioritize what matters most, and achieve greater financial security, freedom, and fulfillment.

CHAPTER SIX

Building Wealth: The Importance of Investing

Investing is a powerful tool for building wealth and achieving financial freedom. While saving money is essential for short-term needs and emergencies, investing allows individuals to grow their wealth over the long term and generate passive income. In this chapter, we will explore the importance of investing, different investment options, strategies for successful investing, and how to get started on the path to financial independence.

Understanding the Importance of Investing

Investing is essential for several reasons:

1. *Wealth Accumulation*: Investing enables individuals to grow their wealth over time by earning returns on their capital. By harnessing the power of compound interest and reinvesting dividends, investors can multiply their initial investment and achieve financial goals faster than through saving alone.
2. *Beating Inflation*: Inflation erodes the purchasing power of money over time, reducing the value of savings held in cash. Investing in assets that outpace inflation, such as stocks, real estate, and commodities, helps preserve and grow wealth over the long term.
3. *Generating Passive Income*: Certain investments, such as dividend-paying stocks, bonds, and rental properties, generate passive income streams that can supplement earned income and provide financial security. By building a diversified investment portfolio, individuals can create multiple streams of passive income to support their lifestyle and

retirement needs.

4. ***Achieving Financial Goals***: Investing allows individuals to achieve financial goals such as retirement, education, homeownership, travel, and philanthropy. By setting clear goals and developing a strategic investment plan, individuals can work towards their objectives and realize their aspirations.

Types of Investments

There are various investment options available, each with its own risk-return profile, liquidity, and investment horizon. Some common types of investments include:

1. ***Stocks***: Stocks represent ownership shares in publicly traded companies. Investing in stocks offers the potential for high returns but also comes with higher volatility and risk. Stocks can be purchased through brokerage accounts or investment funds such as mutual funds and exchange-traded funds (ETFs).
2. ***Bonds***: Bonds are debt securities issued by governments, municipalities, or corporations to raise capital. Investing in bonds provides fixed interest payments over a specified period and offers more stability than stocks. Bonds can be purchased individually or through bond funds.
3. ***Real Estate***: Real estate investments involve purchasing physical properties such as residential or commercial buildings, land, or real estate investment trusts (**REITs**). Real estate offers the potential for appreciation, rental income, and tax benefits but requires active management and carries risks related to market fluctuations and property management.
4. ***Mutual Funds***: Mutual funds pool money from multiple investors to invest in a diversified portfolio of stocks, bonds, or other assets. Mutual funds offer professional management, diversification, and liquidity but typically charge management fees and other expenses.
5. ***Exchange-Traded Funds (ETFs)***: ETFs are similar to mutual funds but trade on stock exchanges like individual stocks. ETFs offer low costs, tax efficiency, and intraday trading flexibility, making them popular investment vehicles for both individual and institutional investors.

6. ***Retirement Accounts***: In the US Retirement accounts such as 401(k) plans, individual retirement accounts (IRAs), and Roth IRAs offer tax advantages for long-term savings and investing.In India National Pension scheme(NPS) offers similar benefits. These accounts allow individuals to invest in a variety of assets and defer taxes on investment gains until retirement.

Strategies for Successful Investing

Successful investing requires a disciplined approach and a long-term perspective. Here are some strategies to consider:

1. ***Set Clear Goals***: Define your investment objectives, time horizon, risk tolerance, and desired rate of return. Tailor your investment strategy to align with your goals and financial circumstances.
2. ***Diversify Your Portfolio***: Diversification is the key to managing risk and maximizing returns. Spread your investments across different asset classes, sectors, and geographic regions to reduce exposure to individual risks and market fluctuations.
3. ***Invest Regularly***: Take advantage of dollar-cost averaging by investing a fixed amount of money at regular intervals, regardless of market conditions. This strategy helps smooth out market volatility and allows you to accumulate shares over time.
4. ***Rebalance Your Portfolio***: Periodically review and rebalance your investment portfolio to maintain the desired asset allocation and risk level. Sell assets that have appreciated and reallocate funds to underperforming assets to restore the desired balance.
5. ***Stay Informed***: Stay informed about market trends, economic indicators, and geopolitical events that may impact your investments. Conduct thorough research and seek advice from trusted financial professionals before making investment decisions.
6. ***Manage Emotions***: Avoid making impulsive decisions based on fear, greed, or market sentiment. Stick to your investment plan and remain disciplined during periods of market volatility or uncertainty.
7. ***Monitor Performance***: Regularly monitor the performance of your investments and evaluate whether they are meeting your expectations. Adjust your investment strategy as needed based on changes in your

financial goals or market conditions.

Getting Started with Investing

Getting started with investing can seem daunting, but it's essential to take the first step towards building wealth. Here are some steps to help you get started:

1. *Educate Yourself*: Take the time to educate yourself about different investment options, strategies, and terminology. Read books, articles, and online resources, attend seminars or workshops, and consider taking investment courses to expand your knowledge.
2. *Assess Your Risk Tolerance*: Understand your risk tolerance and investment objectives before making investment decisions. Consider factors such as your age, investment horizon, financial goals, and comfort level with volatility.
3. *Open an Investment Account*: Open an investment account with a reputable brokerage firm or financial institution. Choose a brokerage platform that offers a wide range of investment options, low fees, user-friendly interface, and research tools.
4. *Start Small*: Start with a small amount of money and gradually increase your investment contributions over time. Consider investing in **low-cost index funds** or **ETFs** as a beginner-friendly option that offers diversification and broad market exposure.
5. *Seek Professional Advice*: Consider seeking advice from a qualified financial advisor or investment professional to help you develop a personalized investment plan based on your goals and risk tolerance. A financial advisor can provide guidance, expertise, and ongoing support to help you navigate the complexities of investing.
6. *Stay Patient and Disciplined*: Investing is a long-term endeavor that requires patience, discipline, and a willingness to ride out market fluctuations. Stay focused on your long-term goals and avoid making impulsive decisions based on short-term market movements.

Learnings

Investing is a powerful tool for building wealth, achieving financial goals, and securing financial independence. By understanding the importance of investing, exploring different investment options, adopting successful investing strategies, and getting started on the path to investing, individuals can take control of their financial future and work towards achieving their dreams. Whether you're saving for a world tour, vacations, retirement, funding your child's education, or building a nest egg for the future, investing offers the potential for growth, income, and financial security. By staying informed, setting clear goals, diversifying your portfolio, and staying disciplined, you can harness the power of investing to build wealth and create a brighter financial future for yourself and your loved ones.

CHAPTER SEVEN

Creating Your Investment Strategy: Setting Goals and Priorities

Investing is not merely about putting money into assets; it's about aligning your financial decisions with your life goals and priorities. Developing a robust investment strategy begins with setting clear objectives and determining where to allocate your resources to achieve those goals. In this chapter, we will delve into the process of creating an investment strategy tailored to your unique aspirations, covering the importance of goal setting, prioritizing objectives, determining risk tolerance, asset allocation strategies, and tips for implementing and monitoring your investment plan effectively.

The Significance of Setting Goals

Setting goals is the cornerstone of any successful investment strategy. Goals provide direction, motivation, and a framework for decision-making. When you have well-defined objectives, you can tailor your investment approach to suit your needs and preferences. Here's why goal setting is crucial:

1. *Clarity and Focus*: Establishing specific, measurable, achievable, relevant, and time-bound (SMART) goals brings clarity to your financial journey. It gives you a clear target to aim for and helps you stay focused amidst distractions or market volatility.
2. *Motivation and Accountability*: Goals serve as a source of motivation, driving you to make consistent efforts towards achieving them. When

you have tangible goals in place, you feel more accountable for your financial decisions and are less likely to deviate from your plan.

3. *Guidance for Decision-Making*: Your goals act as a compass, guiding your investment decisions. Whether you're evaluating different investment opportunities or considering a major financial move, you can assess its alignment with your goals to determine its suitability.

4. *Progress Tracking*: Setting goals allows you to track your progress and celebrate milestones along the way. It provides a sense of accomplishment as you move closer to achieving your objectives and enables you to make course corrections if necessary.

Prioritizing Your Financial Objectives

Once you've identified your financial goals, it's essential to prioritize them based on their importance, urgency, and feasibility. Not all goals are created equal, and some may require moremmediate attention or resources than others. Here are some factors to consider when prioritizing your objectives:

1. *Urgency*: Assess the urgency of each goal based on its **time horizon and importance**. Goals with imminent deadlines or time-sensitive needs may take precedence over longer-term objectives.

2. *Importance*: Consider the significance of each goal in relation to your overall financial well-being and life satisfaction. Some goals, such as retirement savings or debt repayment, may have a higher priority due to their long-term impact on your financial security.

3. *Feasibility*: Evaluate the feasibility of each goal based on your current financial situation, income level, expenses, and available resources. Some goals may require more significant financial commitments or lifestyle adjustments than others, making them more challenging to achieve.

4. *Risk Tolerance*: Take into account your risk tolerance and comfort level with different investment strategies and asset classes. Goals that require higher returns or have longer time horizons may entail greater risk and volatility, whereas more conservative goals may prioritize capital preservation and stability.

Creating Your Investment Strategy

Once you've established your financial goals and priorities, it's time to develop an investment strategy that aligns with your objectives. Your investment strategy should take into account factors such as risk tolerance, time horizon, asset allocation, and diversification. Here's how to create your investment strategy:

1. ***Assess Your Risk Tolerance***: Begin by assessing your risk tolerance, which is your ability and willingness to withstand fluctuations in the value of your investments. Consider factors such as your age, investment experience, financial goals, and comfort with volatility.

2. ***Define Your Investment Objectives***: Clearly define your investment objectives based on your financial goals, time horizon, and risk tolerance. Are you investing for retirement, wealth accumulation, education funding, or other long-term objectives? Your investment objectives will guide your asset allocation and investment decisions.

3. ***Establish Your Asset Allocation***: Determine your optimal asset allocation based on your risk tolerance, investment objectives, and time horizon. Asset allocation refers to the mix of different asset classes, such as stocks, bonds, cash, and real estate, in your investment portfolio. It's essential to strike a balance between growth-oriented assets and more conservative investments to achieve diversification and manage risk.

4. ***Select Your Investments***: Choose specific investments that align with your asset allocation and investment objectives. Consider factors such as investment style, performance history, fees, and tax implications when selecting individual securities or investment funds.

5. ***Implement Your Strategy***: Once you've selected your investments, it's time to implement your investment strategy by funding your accounts and purchasing the chosen assets. Be sure to follow your asset allocation plan and avoid making impulsive changes based on short-term market movements.

6. ***Monitor and Rebalance Your Portfolio***: Regularly monitor your investment portfolio and rebalance it as needed to maintain your desired asset allocation. Rebalancing involves selling overperforming assets and reallocating funds to underperforming assets to restore the target asset allocation. Rebalancing ensures that your portfolio remains aligned with your investment objectives and risk tolerance over time.

7. ***Review and Adjust Your Strategy***: Periodically review your investment strategy and make adjustments as needed based on changes in your financial situation, market conditions, or investment goals. Stay informed about economic trends, market developments, and regulatory changes that may impact your investments. Be flexible and willing to adapt your strategy as circumstances change.

Learnings

Creating an investment strategy that aligns with your goals and priorities is essential for achieving long-term financial success. By setting clear objectives, prioritizing your financial goals, and developing a personalized investment plan, you can take control of your financial future and work towards realizing your dreams.

Whether you're saving for short-term needs, planning for major life events, or investing for retirement, having a well-defined investment strategy provides a roadmap for your financial journey. By assessing your risk tolerance, defining your investment objectives, establishing your asset allocation, selecting appropriate investments, and monitoring your portfolio regularly, you can create a sustainable investment strategy that reflects your aspirations and values.

Remember that investing is a dynamic process that requires ongoing evaluation and adjustment. Stay disciplined, stay focused on your long-term goals, and seek professional advice when needed to navigate the complexities of investing successfully. With a clear vision, a sound strategy, and a commitment to your financial well-being, you can build a brighter future for yourself and your loved ones.

CHAPTER EIGHT

Overcoming Common Investment Pitfalls

Investing can be a rewarding journey towards financial independence and wealth accumulation. However, it's not without its challenges and potential pitfalls. From emotional decision-making to lack of diversification, there are several common mistakes that investors often encounter. In this chapter, we'll explore some of the most prevalent investment pitfalls and provide strategies for overcoming them to achieve long-term success in your investment journey.

Emotional Decision-Making

One of the most common investment pitfalls is succumbing to emotions such as fear, greed, and panic. Emotional decision-making can lead investors to make impulsive or irrational choices that deviate from their long-term investment strategy. To overcome this pitfall, it's essential to:

1. *Stay disciplined*: Stick to your investment plan and resist the temptation to make decisions based on short-term market fluctuations or emotional reactions.
2. *Focus on fundamentals*: Base your investment decisions on sound financial principles, thorough research, and a long-term perspective rather than reacting to market noise or media hype.
3. *Utilize dollar-cost averaging*: Invest a fixed amount of money at regular intervals, regardless of market conditions, to smooth out market volatility and reduce the impact of emotional decision-making.

Lack of Diversification

Failing to diversify your investment portfolio is another common pitfall that can expose you to unnecessary risk. Concentrating your investments in a single asset class, sector, or geographic region increases your vulnerability to adverse market movements. To avoid this pitfall, consider:

1. *Asset allocation*: Spread your investments across different asset classes, such as stocks, bonds, cash, and real estate, to achieve diversification and balance risk.
2. *Sector diversification*: Invest in a variety of industries and sectors to reduce the impact of sector-specific risks and take advantage of opportunities across different sectors of the economy.
3. *Geographic diversification*: Allocate investments across various geographic regions to mitigate the risk of geopolitical events, currency fluctuations, and regional economic downturns.

Chasing Performance

Many investors fall into the trap of chasing past performance, believing that assets or investment strategies that have performed well in the past will continue to do so in the future. However, past performance is not necessarily indicative of future results, and chasing performance can lead to disappointment and underperformance. To overcome this pitfall:

1. *Focus on long-term fundamentals*: Evaluate investments based on their underlying fundamentals, such as earnings growth, revenue potential, and valuation metrics, rather than short-term performance.
2. *Avoid market timing*: Resist the urge to buy or sell investments based on short-term market movements or speculative trends. Instead, maintain a disciplined investment approach focused on your long-term goals and objectives.

Neglecting Risk Management

Failure to adequately assess and manage risk is a significant pitfall that can expose investors to unexpected losses and setbacks. Risk management is an integral part of the investment process and involves identifying, evaluating, and mitigating potential risks. To address this pitfall:

1. *Understand your risk tolerance*: Assess your risk tolerance and investment objectives to determine the appropriate level of risk for your portfolio. Consider factors such as your age, investment horizon, financial goals, and comfort with volatility.
2. *Diversify your portfolio*: Spread your investments across different asset classes, sectors, and geographic regions to reduce concentration risk and minimize the impact of adverse market movements.
3. *Use stop-loss orders*: Implement stop-loss orders to **automatically** sell investments if they reach predetermined price levels, limiting potential losses and protecting against market downturns.
4. *Maintain an emergency fund*: Build an emergency fund with liquid assets to cover unexpected expenses or **financial emergencies**, providing a buffer against market volatility and unforeseen circumstances.

Overlooking Fees and Expenses

Investment fees and expenses can erode your returns over time, reducing the overall performance of your investment portfolio. It's essential to be mindful of fees and expenses associated with investment products and services and seek cost-effective solutions. To mitigate this pitfall:

1. *Compare fees and expenses*: Compare fees and expenses associated with different investment products, such as mutual funds, ETFs, and brokerage accounts, to identify cost-effective options.
2. *Choose low-cost investment vehicles*: Select low-cost investment vehicles, such as **index funds** or ETFs, that offer competitive fees and expense ratios compared to actively managed funds.
3. *Negotiate fees*: Negotiate fees with financial advisors, investment managers, or brokerage firms to potentially lower costs and maximize your investment returns.

Failing to Rebalance Your Portfolio

Failure to rebalance your investment portfolio regularly is another common pitfall that can lead to portfolio drift and unintended risk exposure. Rebalancing involves periodically adjusting your asset allocation to maintain your desired risk-return profile. To address this pitfall:

1. ***Establish a rebalancing strategy***: Develop a systematic approach to rebalancing your portfolio, such as setting predefined thresholds for asset allocation deviations or rebalancing on a scheduled basis (e.g., annually or semi-annually).
2. ***Monitor your portfolio***: Regularly monitor your investment portfolio and review performance against your target asset allocation. Identify deviations from your desired allocation and take appropriate action to rebalance your portfolio.
3. ***Consider tax implications***: Evaluate the tax implications of rebalancing your portfolio, particularly in taxable accounts, and consider tax-efficient strategies to minimize the impact of capital gains taxes.

Learnings

Overcoming common investment pitfalls is essential for achieving long-term success in your investment journey. By staying disciplined, diversifying your portfolio, focusing on fundamentals, managing risk, minimizing fees, and rebalancing your portfolio regularly, you can navigate the complexities of investing with confidence and resilience.

Remember that investing is a marathon, not a sprint, and success often requires patience, discipline, and a long-term perspective. By avoiding common pitfalls and adhering to sound investment principles, you can build wealth steadily over time and achieve your financial goals. Stay informed, stay focused on your objectives, and seek professional advice when needed to make informed investment decisions and maximize your financial potential.

CHAPTER NINE

Investing in Yourself: Education, Skills, and Career Growth

While investing in financial assets is crucial for building wealth, it's equally essential to invest in yourself. Personal and professional development can significantly impact your earning potential, career advancement, and overall financial well-being. In this chapter, we'll explore the importance of investing in education, skills, and career growth, as well as strategies for maximizing the returns on these investments.

The Value of Investing in Yourself

Investing in yourself is one of the most valuable investments you can make. By acquiring new knowledge, developing skills, and advancing your career, you can enhance your earning potential, increase job satisfaction, and open up new opportunities for personal and professional growth. Here's why investing in yourself is essential:

1. *Enhanced Earning Potential*: Continuous learning and skill development can lead to higher-paying job opportunities, promotions, and salary increases. By investing in education and acquiring in-demand skills, you can command higher wages and increase your earning potential over time.

2. *Career Advancement*: Investing in yourself can accelerate your career progression and open doors to new opportunities. Whether through formal education, professional certifications, or networking, expanding

your skill set and knowledge base can position you for leadership roles, managerial positions, and career advancement opportunities.

3. ***Adaptability and Resilience***: In today's rapidly changing job market, adaptability and resilience are essential qualities for success. Investing in yourself allows you to stay relevant, agile, and adaptable in the face of technological advancements, industry disruptions, and evolving job requirements.

4. ***Personal Fulfillment***: Investing in yourself is not just about financial gain; it's also about personal fulfillment and self-improvement. Pursuing interests, hobbies, and passions through education and skill development can enrich your life, boost your self-confidence, and enhance your overall well-being.

Strategies for Investing in Yourself

There are various ways to invest in yourself, ranging from formal education and professional development to personal growth and wellness activities. Here are some strategies for investing in yourself effectively:

1. ***Continuous Learning***: Commit to lifelong learning and personal development by seeking out opportunities to acquire new knowledge and skills. This could involve enrolling in courses, attending workshops, reading books, or taking online classes on topics relevant to your interests and career goals.

2. ***Formal Education***: Consider pursuing higher education, such as a degree program or specialized certification, to enhance your credentials and qualifications. Whether through traditional universities, online institutions, or vocational schools, formal education can provide valuable knowledge, credentials, and networking opportunities.

3. ***Professional Certifications***: Obtain industry-recognized certifications or credentials to demonstrate your expertise and competency in your field. Professional certifications can enhance your credibility, marketability, and earning potential, particularly in specialized or technical fields.

4. ***Skill Development***: Identify areas for skill development and focus on acquiring skills that are in demand in your industry or profession. This could include technical skills, soft skills, leadership skills, or specialized competencies relevant to your career objectives.

5. ***Networking and Relationship Building***: Invest in building professional relationships and expanding your network through networking events, industry conferences, and professional associations. Networking can provide access to job opportunities, mentorship, and valuable connections that can support your career growth.
6. ***Personal Growth and Wellness***: Don't neglect your personal growth and well-being in pursuit of professional success. Invest in activities that promote physical health, mental well-being, and work-life balance, such as exercise, meditation, hobbies, and time spent with loved ones.

Maximizing the Returns on Your Investments

To maximize the returns on your investments in education, skills, and career growth, it's essential to approach these endeavors strategically and with a long-term perspective. Here are some tips for maximizing the returns on your investments in yourself:

1. ***Set Clear Goals***: Define your personal and professional goals and align your investments in education, skills, and career growth with these objectives. Having clear goals will guide your decision-making and keep you focused on what matters most to you.
2. ***Prioritize Your Investments***: Assess your strengths, weaknesses, and areas for improvement to prioritize your investments in education and skill development. Focus on acquiring skills and knowledge that are relevant to your career goals and have the potential to provide the greatest return on investment.
3. ***Seek Feedback and Mentorship***: Solicit feedback from peers, supervisors, mentors, and industry experts to identify areas for improvement and opportunities for growth. Actively seek out mentorship and guidance from experienced professionals who can provide valuable insights and advice.
4. ***Stay Current and Adapt***: Stay abreast of industry trends, technological advancements, and changes in the job market to remain competitive and relevant. Be willing to adapt and evolve your skills and knowledge to meet the evolving demands of your profession and industry.
5. ***Network Strategically***: Invest time and effort in building and nurturing professional relationships that can support your career growth and

advancement. Be proactive in networking, attending industry events, and cultivating relationships with peers, mentors, and potential employers.

6. ***Measure Your Progress***: Regularly assess your progress towards your personal and professional goals and adjust your investments and strategies as needed. Track your achievements, milestones, and areas for improvement to ensure that you're making meaningful progress towards your objectives.

Learnings

Investing in yourself is a powerful strategy for achieving personal and professional success. By committing to continuous learning, skill development, and career growth, you can enhance your earning potential, advance your career, and lead a more fulfilling life. Whether through formal education, professional certifications, skill development, or personal growth activities, investing in yourself is an investment that pays dividends for a lifetime.

Remember that investing in yourself is not a one-time event but an ongoing journey of growth and self-improvement. Stay curious, stay hungry for knowledge, and stay committed to your personal and professional development. By investing in yourself today, you're laying the foundation for a brighter and more prosperous future tomorrow.

CHAPTER TEN

Harnessing the Power of Compounding: Making Money Work for You

One of the most potent forces in finance is compound interest. When utilized effectively, compound interest can significantly amplify your wealth over time, allowing your money to work for you and grow exponentially. In this chapter, we will delve into the concept of compound interest, its mechanics, and strategies for harnessing its power to achieve your financial goals.

Understanding Compound Interest

Compound interest is the process of earning interest on both the initial principal and the accumulated interest of an investment. Unlike simple interest, which is calculated only on the principal amount, compound interest allows your money to grow exponentially over time. The key components of compound interest include:

1. *Principal*: The initial amount of money invested or deposited.
2. *Interest Rate*: The annual rate at which interest is earned on the investment.
3. *Time*: The length of time over which the investment grows.
4. The formula for calculating compound interest is: $A = P \times (1+r)^n$. Where: A is the future value of the investment; P is the initial principal or investment amount; r is the annual interest rate (expressed as a decimal); n is the number of compounding periods (e.g., the number of years or

the frequency of compounding).

The Power of Compounding

The **magic of compound interest** lies in its ability to generate **exponential growth** over time. As interest is earned not only on the initial principal but also on the accumulated interest, the growth of the investment accelerates with each compounding period. The longer the investment horizon and the higher the interest rate, the greater the impact of compounding.

Consider the following example: Suppose you invest $1,000 in a savings account with an annual interest rate of 5%, compounded annually. After one year, your investment grows to $1,050. In the second year, you earn interest not only on the initial $1,000 but also on the $50 of accumulated interest from the first year. Over time, this compounding effect snowballs, resulting in exponential growth of your investment.

Strategies for Harnessing Compound Interest

To harness the power of compound interest effectively, it's essential to adopt strategies that maximize its benefits and optimize your investment returns. Here are some strategies for making compound interest work for you:

1. *Start Early*: The most **critical** factor in maximizing the power of compound interest is time. The earlier you start investing, the more time your money has to compound and grow. Even small amounts invested consistently over a long period can result in significant wealth accumulation due to the exponential growth of compound interest.

2. *Invest Regularly*: Consistent contributions to your investment accounts, such as retirement accounts, brokerage accounts, or savings accounts, can amplify the effects of compound interest. Set up automatic contributions or savngs plans to ensure that you're regularly adding to your investments and taking advantage of compounding.

3. *Reinvest Dividends and Interest*: Instead of withdrawing dividends or interest earned on your investments, consider reinvesting them to allow for greater compounding over time. Reinvesting dividends and interest can accelerate the growth of your investment portfolio and magnify its

long-term returns.

4. ***Choose High-Quality Investments***: Select investments with strong growth potential, such as stocks, mutual funds, or exchange-traded funds (ETFs), to capitalize on the power of compound interest. While these investments may carry higher risk than more conservative options, they also offer the potential for higher returns and greater compounding over time.

5. ***Take Advantage of Tax-Advantaged Accounts***: Invest in tax-advantaged accounts, such as retirement accounts (e.g., 401(k), IRA) or education savings accounts (e.g., 529 plan), to maximize the benefits of compound interest. These accounts offer tax-deferred or tax-free growth, allowing your investments to compound more efficiently without being eroded by taxes.

6. ***Diversify Your Portfolio***: Maintain a diversified investment portfolio to spread risk and capture growth opportunities across different asset classes and sectors. Diversification can help mitigate the impact of market fluctuations and enhance the long-term performance of your investments, further amplifying the effects of compound interest.

7. ***Monitor and Rebalance Your Portfolio***: Regularly review your investment portfolio and rebalance it as needed to maintain your desired asset allocation and risk profile. Rebalancing ensures that your investments remain aligned with your financial goals and objectives, optimizing the compounding effect over time.

Real-Life Examples of Compound Interest

To illustrate the power of compound interest, let's consider a few real-life examples:

1. ***Retirement Savings***: Suppose you start investing $500 per month in a retirement account at age 25, with an average annual return of 7%. By the time you reach age 65, your investment would have grown to over $1 million, thanks to the compounding effect of interest over 40 years.

2. ***College Savings***: If you invest $100 per month in a 529 college savings plan for your child from birth until age 18, with an average annual return of 6%, you would accumulate over $45,000 by the time your child is ready for college, primarily due to compound interest.

3. ***Debt Repayment***: Conversely, compound interest can work against you when it comes to debt. For example, carrying a credit card balance with an annual interest rate of 20% can quickly balloon over time due to compound interest, making it challenging to pay off the debt.

Learnings

Compound interest is a powerful tool for building wealth and achieving financial freedom. By understanding the mechanics of compound interest and implementing strategies to harness its power effectively, you can make your money work for you and accelerate your journey towards your financial goals.

Whether you're saving for retirement, funding your child's education, or building a nest egg for the future, compound interest can amplify your efforts and lead to exponential growth over time. Start early, invest regularly, and take advantage of tax-advantaged accounts and diversified investments to maximize the benefits of compound interest and secure your financial future. With patience, discipline, and a long-term perspective, you can harness the power of compound interest to achieve your dreams and build a brighter financial future for yourself and your loved ones.

CHAPTER ELEVEN

The Role of Patience and Discipline in Investing

Investing is often portrayed as a fast-paced and dynamic endeavor, with the potential for quick profits and rapid wealth accumulation. However, the reality is that successful investing requires patience, discipline, and a long-term perspective. In this chapter, we'll explore the crucial role of patience and discipline in investing, why they are essential for achieving long-term financial success, and strategies for cultivating these virtues in your investment approach.

The Importance of Patience

Patience is a fundamental attribute of successful investors. It involves the ability to remain calm and composed in the face of market volatility, resist the temptation to make impulsive decisions, and stay committed to your long-term investment strategy. Here's why patience is crucial in investing:

1. *Riding Out Market Volatility*: Financial markets are inherently volatile, with prices fluctuating based on a myriad of factors, including economic data, geopolitical events, and investor sentiment. Patience allows investors to withstand market fluctuations without succumbing to panic or making hasty investment decisions based on short-term movements.

2. *Achieving Long-Term Growth*: The power of compounding, as discussed in previous chapters, requires time to realize its full potential. Patient investors understand that wealth accumulation is a gradual process that requires consistent contributions, disciplined saving habits, and a long-term investment horizon.

3. ***Avoiding Emotional Decision-Making***: Emotional decision-making, driven by fear, greed, or FOMO (fear of missing out), can lead to costly mistakes and undermine investment performance. Patience enables investors to maintain a rational and objective approach to investing, focusing on fundamental principles rather than succumbing to emotional impulses.

4. ***Taking Advantage of Opportunities***: Patient investors have the discipline to wait for attractive investment opportunities to arise, rather than chasing hot trends or trying to time the market. By exercising patience, investors can capitalize on undervalued assets, market downturns, or temporary setbacks to build positions at favorable prices.

The Role of Discipline

Discipline is another essential trait for successful investing. It involves sticking to your investment plan, adhering to predefined rules and principles, and resisting the temptation to deviate from your long-term strategy. Here's why discipline is crucial in investing:

1. ***Sticking to Your Investment Plan***: A well-thought-out investment plan serves as a roadmap for achieving your financial goals. Discipline is essential for sticking to your plan, maintaining consistency in your investment approach, and avoiding impulsive or emotional decisions that deviate from your strategy.

2. ***Consistent Saving and Investing***: Discipline is required to consistently save and invest a portion of your income, regardless of market conditions or short-term fluctuations. Regular contributions to your investment accounts, such as retirement accounts or brokerage accounts, are essential for harnessing the power of compounding and achieving long-term growth.

3. ***Resisting Market Noise***: Financial markets are inundated with noise, including media headlines, market rumors, and speculative trends. Discipline allows investors to filter out the noise and focus on long-term fundamentals, avoiding knee-jerk reactions to short-term market movements or sensationalized news.

Strategies for Cultivating Patience and Discipline

Cultivating patience and discipline requires conscious effort and practice. Here are some strategies for developing these virtues in your investment approach:

1. *Set Clear Goals*: Define your investment goals, objectives, and time horizon to provide a framework for your investment strategy. Having clear goals helps maintain focus and discipline during periods of market volatility or uncertainty.
2. *Create an Investment Plan*: Develop a comprehensive investment plan that outlines your asset allocation, diversification strategy, risk tolerance, and rebalancing criteria. Stick to your plan and resist the temptation to deviate from it based on short-term market fluctuations.
3. *Automate Your Investments*: Automate contributions to your investment accounts, such as setting up automatic transfers or payroll deductions, to ensure consistent saving and investing. Automation removes the temptation to time the market or make emotional decisions based on market movements.
4. *Practice Mindfulness*: Cultivate mindfulness and self-awareness to recognize and manage emotional triggers that may lead to impulsive investment decisions. Practice techniques such as deep breathing, meditation, or journaling to stay grounded and maintain perspective during periods of market volatility.
5. *Stay Informed, But Not Overwhelmed*: Stay informed about economic trends, market developments, and investment opportunities, but avoid becoming overwhelmed by excessive information or noise. Focus on high-quality sources of information and filter out distractions that may detract from your long-term investment strategy.

Learnings

Patience and discipline are essential virtues for successful investing. By cultivating these qualities in your investment approach, you can navigate market volatility, stay focused on your long-term goals, and achieve financial success over time. Remember that investing is a marathon, not a sprint, and success often requires patience, discipline, and a long-term perspective. Stay committed to your investment plan, stick to your predefined rules and principles, and trust in the power of compounding to grow your wealth steadily over time. With patience and discipline as your guiding principles, you can build a solid foundation for financial security and achieve your dreams for the future.

CHAPTER TWELVE

Leveraging Technology for Financial Management and Investing

In today's digital age, technology has revolutionized the way we manage our finances and invest our money. From mobile banking apps to robo-advisors, there is a wide range of technological tools and platforms available to help individuals achieve their financial goals more efficiently and effectively. In this chapter, we'll explore the various ways in which technology can be leveraged for financial management and investing, empowering individuals to take control of their finances and build wealth for the future.

Online Banking and Personal Finance Apps

Online banking and personal finance apps have transformed the way individuals manage their day-to-day finances. These digital tools allow users to access their bank accounts, track spending, set budgeting goals, and monitor transactions from the convenience of their smartphones or computers. Key features of online banking and personal finance apps include:

1. *Account Aggregation*: Consolidate all your financial accounts, including bank accounts, credit cards, loans, and investments, in one centralized dashboard for easy monitoring and management.
2. *Budgeting and Expense Tracking*: Set budgeting goals, track spending habits, and categorize expenses to gain insights into your financial behavior and identify areas for saving or cutting back.

3. **Bill Payment and Transfers**: Schedule bill payments, transfer funds between accounts, and set up recurring transactions to automate routine financial tasks and avoid late fees.
4. **Alerts and Notifications**: Receive real-time alerts and notifications for account balances, upcoming payments, suspicious transactions, or budgeting milestones to stay informed and proactive about your finances.

Popular online banking and personal finance apps include Mint, YNAB (You Need a Budget), Personal Capital, and Quicken.

Robo-Advisors and Automated Investing Platforms

Robo-advisors and automated investing platforms leverage technology and algorithms to provide personalized investment advice and portfolio management services at a fraction of the cost of traditional financial advisors. These platforms use algorithms to assess investors' risk tolerance, investment goals, and time horizon, then recommend a diversified portfolio of low-cost exchange-traded funds (ETFs) or mutual funds tailored to their individual needs. Key features of robo-advisors and automated investing platforms include:

1. **Automated Portfolio Management**: Build and manage a diversified investment portfolio tailored to your risk tolerance, financial goals, and time horizon without the need for manual intervention.
2. **Tax-Loss Harvesting**: Utilize tax-efficient investment strategies, such as tax-loss harvesting, to minimize tax liabilities and optimize after-tax returns.
3. **Low Fees**: Benefit from lower fees compared to traditional financial advisors, as robo-advisors typically charge a fraction of the fees associated with human advisors.
4. **Accessibility and Convenience**: Access your investment portfolio and monitor performance through user-friendly interfaces and mobile apps, making it easy to track progress and make adjustments as needed.

Popular robo-advisors and automated investing platforms include Betterment, Wealthfront, Vanguard Personal Advisor Services, and Schwab Intelligent Portfolios.

Financial Education and Learning Platforms

Technology has democratized access to financial education and learning resources, allowing individuals to expand their knowledge of personal finance, investing, and wealth management at their own pace and convenience. Online courses, webinars, podcasts, and blogs provide valuable insights and practical tips on a wide range of financial topics, empowering individuals to make informed decisions about their money. Key features of financial education and learning platforms include:

1. *Comprehensive Curriculum*: Access a wide range of educational resources covering topics such as budgeting, saving, investing, retirement planning, tax strategies, and estate planning to gain a holistic understanding of personal finance.
2. *Expert Insights*: Learn from industry experts, financial professionals, and seasoned investors who share their knowledge, experiences, and best practices through online courses, podcasts, and webinars.
3. *Interactive Tools and Calculators*: Utilize interactive tools, calculators, and quizzes to assess your financial situation, set goals, and develop actionable plans for achieving financial success.
4. *Community and Support*: Connect with like-minded individuals, participate in discussion forums, and seek guidance from mentors or financial advisors to enhance your learning experience and receive personalized advice.

Popular financial education and learning platforms include Investopedia, Khan Academy, Udemy, Coursera, and The Motley Fool.

Investment Research and Analysis Tools

Technology has democratized access to investment research and analysis tools, enabling individuals to conduct thorough due diligence and make informed investment decisions. Online brokerage platforms, financial news websites, and investment research portals provide access to real-time market data, research reports, analyst ratings, and investment analysis tools to help investors evaluate investment opportunities and build diversified portfolios. Key features of investment research and analysis tools include:

1. ***Market Data and Insights***: Access real-time market data, news updates, and economic indicators to stay informed about market trends, developments, and opportunities.
2. ***Research Reports and Analysis***: Review research reports, company profiles, and investment analysis from reputable sources to assess the fundamentals, valuation, and growth prospects of individual stocks or ETFs.
3. ***Technical Analysis Tools***: Utilize technical analysis tools, charts, and indicators to identify trends, patterns, and potential entry or exit points for trading or investment decisions.
4. ***Portfolio Tracking and Performance Analysis***: Track the performance of your investment portfolio, analyze asset allocation, and evaluate risk-adjusted returns using portfolio tracking and performance analysis tools.

Popular investment research and analysis tools include Bloomberg, Morningstar, Yahoo Finance, Google Finance, and StockCharts.

Learnings

Technology has transformed the landscape of financial management and investing, empowering individuals with unprecedented access to tools, resources, and platforms to manage their finances, make informed investment decisions, and build wealth for the future. From online banking and personal finance apps to robo-advisors, financial education platforms, and investment research tools, technology has democratized access to financial services and leveled the playing field for individual investors.

By leveraging technology effectively, individuals can take control of their financial futures, achieve their investment goals, and navigate the complexities of today's financial markets with confidence and convenience. Whether you're tracking expenses, building a diversified investment portfolio, learning about personal finance concepts, or conducting investment research, technology offers a wealth of opportunities to enhance your financial literacy, optimize your investment strategy, and maximize your long-term wealth accumulation. Embrace the power of technology to empower yourself financially and embark on a journey toward financial success and independence.

CHAPTER THIRTEEN

Sustainable and Ethical Investing: Aligning Your Values with Your Portfolio

In recent years, there has been a growing trend towards sustainable and ethical investing, as investors increasingly seek to align their financial goals with their values and beliefs. Sustainable and ethical investing, also known as socially responsible investing (SRI) or environmental, social, and governance (ESG) investing, involves integrating environmental, social, and ethical criteria into investment decisions, alongside traditional financial considerations. In this chapter, we'll explore the principles of sustainable and ethical investing, the benefits it offers, and strategies for incorporating these principles into your investment portfolio.

Understanding Sustainable and Ethical Investing

Sustainable and ethical investing seeks to generate financial returns while also making a positive impact on society, the environment, and corporate governance practices. This approach recognizes that companies and investments have broader social and environmental implications beyond financial performance alone. Sustainable and ethical investors prioritize companies and investments that demonstrate strong environmental stewardship, social responsibility, and ethical business practices.

Key Principles of Sustainable and Ethical Investing:

1. ***Environmental Sustainability***: Sustainable and ethical investors evaluate companies based on their environmental impact and sustainability

practices. They favor companies that demonstrate a commitment to environmental conservation, resource efficiency, renewable energy, and climate change mitigation.

2. ***Social Responsibility***: Socially responsible investors consider a company's social impact, including its treatment of employees, customers, suppliers, and communities. They prioritize companies that promote diversity and inclusion, uphold labor rights, support community development, and contribute positively to society.

3. ***Governance Practices***: Investors assess companies' governance practices, including board diversity, executive compensation, shareholder rights, and transparency. They favor companies with strong corporate governance structures, independent boards of directors, and ethical leadership.

Benefits of Sustainable and Ethical Investing

Sustainable and ethical investing offers several benefits for investors, beyond just financial returns:

1. ***Alignment with Values***: Sustainable and ethical investing allows investors to align their investment decisions with their personal values, beliefs, and ethical considerations. By investing in companies that reflect their values, investors can feel a sense of purpose and satisfaction in knowing that their money is supporting causes they care about.

2. ***Risk Management***: Companies with strong environmental, social, and governance (ESG) practices tend to be more resilient and better equipped to manage risks, such as regulatory changes, reputational damage, and operational disruptions. Sustainable investing can help mitigate risks associated with environmental liabilities, social controversies, and governance failures.

3. ***Long-Term Performance***: Research has shown that companies with strong ESG performance often outperform their peers over the long term. By integrating ESG criteria into investment decisions, investors can potentially enhance their risk-adjusted returns and achieve competitive financial performance while also making a positive impact on society and the environment.

Strategies for Incorporating Sustainable and Ethical Investing

There are several strategies for incorporating sustainable and ethical investing principles into your investment portfolio:

1. ***ESG Integration***: Integrate environmental, social, and governance (ESG) criteria into your investment analysis and decision-making process. Evaluate companies based on their ESG performance and select investments that meet predefined sustainability criteria.
2. ***Screening***: Use positive or negative screening criteria to identify investments that align with your values and exclude companies involved in controversial industries or activities. Positive screening focuses on selecting companies with strong ESG performance, while negative screening excludes companies engaged in activities such as fossil fuel extraction, tobacco production, or weapons manufacturing.
3. ***Thematic Investing***: Invest in thematic funds or strategies that focus on specific sustainability themes or impact areas, such as clean energy, renewable resources, gender equality, or social justice. Thematic investing allows investors to target specific sustainability goals and support companies that are driving positive change in those areas.
4. ***Impact Investing***: Allocate a portion of your portfolio to impact investments that seek to generate measurable social or environmental benefits alongside financial returns. Impact investments may include investments in affordable housing, clean technology, sustainable agriculture, or community development projects.
5. ***Engagement and Advocacy***: Engage with companies, asset managers, and policymakers on ESG issues through shareholder engagement, proxy voting, and advocacy initiatives. Use your voice as a shareholder to advocate for greater transparency, accountability, and responsible business practices.

Learnings

Sustainable and ethical investing represents a powerful opportunity for investors to align their financial goals with their values and beliefs while also making a positive impact on society and the environment. By integrating environmental, social, and governance (ESG) criteria into investment decisions, investors can generate competitive financial returns while promoting sustainability, social responsibility, and ethical business practices.

Whether through ESG integration, screening, thematic investing, impact investing, or engagement and advocacy, there are various strategies for incorporating sustainable and ethical investing principles into your investment portfolio. By taking a proactive approach to sustainable and ethical investing, investors can drive positive change, mitigate risks, and achieve their financial goals in a manner that reflects their values and contributes to a more sustainable and equitable world. Embrace the power of sustainable and ethical investing to create a brighter future for generations to come.

CHAPTER FOURTEEN

Real Estate Investing: Exploring Opportunities Beyond Stocks and Bonds

Real estate investing offers a compelling opportunity for diversification and wealth accumulation beyond traditional stocks and bonds. From rental properties to real estate investment trusts (REITs) and real estate crowdfunding platforms, there are various avenues for individuals to invest in the real estate market and capitalize on its potential for long-term growth and income generation. In this chapter, we'll explore the fundamentals of real estate investing, the benefits it offers, and strategies for incorporating real estate into your investment portfolio.

Understanding Real Estate Investing

Real estate investing involves acquiring, owning, and managing properties with the expectation of generating income and/or capital appreciation over time. Unlike stocks and bonds, which represent ownership in companies or debt obligations, real estate investments provide tangible assets in the form of land, buildings, or other physical properties. Real estate can be categorized into various asset classes, including residential, commercial, industrial, and retail properties, each with its own risk-return profile and investment characteristics.

Key Benefits of Real Estate Investing

Real estate investing offers several unique benefits for investors:

1. *Income Generation*: One of the primary attractions of real estate investing is its potential to generate steady and predictable income through rental payments. Rental properties can provide a reliable source of cash flow, which can be used to cover expenses, reinvest in additional properties, or supplement other sources of income.

2. *Appreciation Potential*: Real estate has historically appreciated in value over the long term, driven by factors such as population growth, economic expansion, and inflation. While property values may fluctuate in the short term, real estate investments have the potential to appreciate significantly over time, providing capital appreciation and wealth accumulation for investors.

3. *Diversification*: Real estate investments offer diversification benefits by providing exposure to an asset class that is not highly correlated with traditional stocks and bonds. Adding real estate to an investment portfolio can help reduce overall portfolio volatility and enhance risk-adjusted returns by spreading risk across different asset classes and market sectors.

4. *Inflation Hedge*: Real estate investments can serve as a hedge against inflation, as property values and rental income tend to increase in line with inflationary pressures over time. Real assets such as real estate have intrinsic value and can help preserve purchasing power during periods of rising prices.

5. *Tax Advantages*: Real estate investing offers various tax advantages, including deductions for mortgage interest, property taxes, depreciation, and operating expenses. Additionally, real estate investors may benefit from favorable tax treatment on capital gains, rental income, and property exchanges.

Strategies for Real Estate Investing

There are several strategies for incorporating real estate into your investment portfolio:

1. *Direct Ownership*: Direct ownership of rental properties involves purchasing residential, commercial, or multifamily properties and renting them out to tenants. This strategy allows investors to generate rental income, benefit from property appreciation, and have direct

control over property management and operations.

2. ***Real Estate Investment Trusts (REITs)***: REITs are publicly traded companies that own, operate, or finance income-producing real estate properties. By investing in REITs, investors can gain exposure to a diversified portfolio of real estate assets, including office buildings, shopping centers, apartments, and hotels, without the need for direct ownership or management responsibilities. REITs offer liquidity, diversification, and potential dividend income, making them an attractive option for passive real estate investors.

3. ***Real Estate Crowdfunding***: Real estate crowdfunding platforms allow investors to pool their capital with other investors to finance real estate projects, such as residential developments, commercial properties, or renovation projects. Crowdfunding platforms provide access to a wide range of investment opportunities, typically with lower investment minimums and reduced barriers to entry compared to traditional real estate investments.

4. ***Real Estate Syndication***: Real estate syndication involves pooling capital from multiple investors to acquire or develop larger real estate projects that may be beyond the reach of individual investors. Syndicators, also known as sponsors or operators, identify and manage investment opportunities on behalf of investors, providing expertise, deal sourcing, and asset management services in exchange for a share of the profits.

5. ***Real Estate Investment Partnerships***: Real estate investment partnerships allow investors to collaborate with others to jointly own and operate real estate properties. Partnerships may take various forms, including joint ventures, limited partnerships, or limited liability companies (LLCs), and offer investors the opportunity to leverage their collective resources, expertise, and networks to pursue larger or more complex real estate investments.

Risks and Considerations

While real estate investing offers attractive benefits, it also comes with certain risks and considerations:

1. ***Market Risk***: Real estate values and rental income may be subject to market fluctuations, economic downturns, and local market conditions.

Investors should carefully assess market dynamics, supply and demand trends, and economic indicators when evaluating real estate investment opportunities.

2. ***Liquidity Risk***: Unlike publicly traded stocks and bonds, real estate investments typically have lower liquidity and may be more challenging to sell or liquidate quickly, particularly during periods of market distress or economic uncertainty. Investors should be prepared for potential liquidity constraints and consider their investment horizon when investing in real estate.

3. ***Management Risk***: Direct ownership of rental properties requires active management and involvement in property maintenance, tenant relations, and financial administration. Investors should be prepared to devote time, resources, and expertise to effectively manage their real estate investments or consider outsourcing management responsibilities to professional property managers.

4. ***Regulatory and Legal Risks***: Real estate investments are subject to various regulatory and legal risks, including zoning regulations, building codes, environmental regulations, landlord-tenant laws, and contractual obligations. Investors should conduct thorough due diligence, seek legal counsel, and understand the regulatory environment before investing in real estate.

5. ***Financing Risk***: Real estate investments often involve leverage, such as mortgage debt, which can magnify returns but also increase financial risk. Investors should carefully evaluate financing options, assess debt service obligations, and consider the potential impact of interest rate fluctuations on investment returns.

Learnings

Real estate investing offers a compelling opportunity for individuals to diversify their investment portfolios, generate income, and build wealth over the long term. Whether through direct ownership of rental properties, investment in REITs, participation in real estate crowdfunding, or collaboration with other investors through syndication or partnerships, there are various avenues for individuals to access the potential benefits of real estate investing.

While real estate investing can offer attractive returns and diversification benefits, it also comes with certain risks and considerations that investors should carefully evaluate. By conducting thorough due diligence, diversifying across different real estate assets, and aligning investments with their financial goals and risk tolerance, investors can effectively incorporate real estate into their investment portfolios and capitalize on its potential for long-term growth and income generation. Embrace the opportunities of real estate investing to enhance your financial well-being and achieve your investment objectives.

CHAPTER FIFTEEN

Entrepreneurship and Side Hustles: Building Additional Streams of Income

In today's dynamic and fast-paced economy, entrepreneurship and side hustles have emerged as popular avenues for individuals to supplement their income, pursue their passions, and build long-term wealth. Whether it's starting a small business, freelancing, or monetizing a hobby or skill, entrepreneurship offers opportunities for creativity, autonomy, and financial independence. In this chapter, we'll explore the benefits of entrepreneurship and side hustles, strategies for getting started, and tips for building additional streams of income.

Understanding Entrepreneurship and Side Hustles

Entrepreneurship refers to the process of identifying, creating, and capturing value through the development of new products, services, or business ventures. Entrepreneurs are innovative, resourceful, and resilient individuals who are willing to take risks and pursue opportunities to create wealth and make a positive impact on society.

Side hustles, on the other hand, are income-generating activities that individuals pursue in addition to their primary source of income, such as a full-time job or business. Side hustles can take various forms, including freelance work, consulting gigs, part-time jobs, or small business ventures, and offer flexibility, autonomy, and supplemental income for individuals looking to diversify their earnings.

Benefits of Entrepreneurship and Side Hustles

Entrepreneurship and side hustles offer several benefits for individuals seeking additional streams of income:

1. *Income Diversification*: Entrepreneurship and side hustles provide an opportunity to diversify sources of income, reducing reliance on a single source of revenue, such as a salary or wages. Diversification can enhance financial stability and resilience, particularly during economic downturns or job market uncertainties.
2. *Flexibility and Autonomy*: Entrepreneurship and side hustles offer flexibility and autonomy to set your own schedule, work on projects that interest you, and pursue your passions outside of traditional employment constraints. Whether you're a freelancer, consultant, or small business owner, entrepreneurship allows you to control your workload, client base, and work environment.
3. *Skill Development*: Entrepreneurship and side hustles provide opportunities for skill development, learning, and personal growth. Whether it's honing your business acumen, developing technical skills, or enhancing interpersonal skills, entrepreneurship offers a hands-on learning experience that can benefit you professionally and personally.
4. *Wealth Building*: Entrepreneurship and side hustles have the potential to generate additional income and build long-term wealth through business ownership, asset accumulation, and investment opportunities. Successful entrepreneurs can create scalable business models, generate passive income streams, and achieve financial independence over time.
5. *Creativity and Innovation*: Entrepreneurship encourages creativity, innovation, and problem-solving as individuals identify market opportunities, develop unique value propositions, and differentiate their products or services from competitors. Entrepreneurs have the freedom to explore new ideas, experiment with different business models, and pursue innovative solutions to address customer needs.

Strategies for Getting Started

If you're considering entrepreneurship or starting a side hustle, here are some strategies to help you get started:

1. ***Identify Your Passion and Skills***: Start by identifying your passions, interests, and skills that you can leverage to create value for others. Consider your hobbies, talents, professional expertise, and areas of expertise that align with market demand and customer needs.
2. ***Validate Your Idea***: Validate your business idea or side hustle concept by conducting market research, assessing competition, and gathering feedback from potential customers or target audience. Determine if there is a demand for your product or service, identify your target market, and evaluate the viability of your business model.
3. ***Create a Business Plan***: Develop a comprehensive business plan that outlines your goals, objectives, target market, value proposition, competitive analysis, marketing strategy, operational plan, and financial projections. A well-thought-out business plan serves as a roadmap for launching and growing your business and provides clarity and direction for your entrepreneurial journey.
4. ***Start Small and Iterate***: Start small and test your business idea or side hustle on a small scale before committing significant resources or capital. Experiment with different strategies, pricing models, and marketing tactics, and iterate based on customer feedback and market response. Embrace a mindset of continuous learning and improvement as you navigate the challenges of entrepreneurship.
5. ***Build Your Brand and Online Presence***: Invest in building your brand identity and online presence through a professional website, social media profiles, and digital marketing channels. Establish credibility, visibility, and brand awareness in your niche market, and leverage online platforms to reach and engage with your target audience.

Tips for Building Additional Streams of Income

In addition to starting a business or side hustle, here are some tips for building additional streams of income:

1. ***Freelancing and Consulting***: Offer your skills and expertise as a freelance contractor or consultant in your field of expertise. Freelancing allows you to work on a flexible basis, take on projects that interest you, and earn income from multiple clients or sources.

2. ***Passive Income Opportunities***: Explore opportunities for generating passive income, such as rental properties, dividend-paying stocks, peer-to-peer lending, or affiliate marketing. Passive income streams can provide ongoing revenue with minimal ongoing effort or active involvement.

3. ***Monetize Your Skills and Talents***: Monetize your skills, talents, and hobbies by offering products or services that people are willing to pay for. Whether it's teaching a skill, creating digital products, offering online courses, or selling andmade crafts, there are various ways to monetize your passions and talents.

4. ***Create Multiple Revenue Streams***: Diversify your income streams by creating multiple revenue streams from different sources, such as e-commerce sales, membership subscriptions, advertising revenue, or affiliate commissions. Multiple revenue streams can provide stability, resilience, and growth opportunities for your business or side hustle.

5. ***Invest in Yourself***: Invest in your personal and professional development by acquiring new skills, knowledge, and certifications that enhance your marketability and earning potential. Continuous learning and skill-building can open up new opportunities for career advancement, higher income, and entrepreneurial success.

Learnings

Entrepreneurship and side hustles offer individuals the opportunity to build additional streams of income, pursue their passions, and achieve financial independence. Whether it's starting a small business, freelancing, or monetizing a hobby, entrepreneurship allows individuals to leverage their skills, creativity, and initiative to create value and generate income on their terms.

By identifying opportunities, validating ideas, creating a plan, and taking action, aspiring entrepreneurs can embark on a rewarding journey of entrepreneurship and build successful businesses or side hustles that align with their goals and aspirations. Embrace the possibilities of entrepreneurship and side hustles to unlock new opportunities, pursue your passions, and create a brighter financial future for yourself and your loved ones.

CHAPTER SIXTEEN

Navigating Economic Challenges: Strategies for Financial Resilience

In today's rapidly changing economic landscape, individuals and families are increasingly faced with various challenges and uncertainties, from economic downturns and job loss to inflation and market volatility. Navigating these economic challenges requires resilience, adaptability, and proactive financial planning to safeguard against potential risks and build long-term financial stability. In this chapter, we'll explore strategies for enhancing financial resilience and weathering economic storms effectively.

Understanding Economic Challenges

Economic challenges can arise from various factors, including changes in the business cycle, fluctuations in the stock market, shifts in consumer behavior, geopolitical tensions, natural disasters, and global pandemics. These challenges can impact individuals and households in different ways, such as job loss, income reduction, increased expenses, investment losses, or changes in purchasing power.

Key Economic Challenges:

1. *Unemployment and Job Insecurity*: Economic downturns and structural changes in industries can lead to job loss, layoffs, or reduced work hours for individuals and families. Unemployment and job insecurity can disrupt financial stability, erode savings, and create uncertainty about future income prospects.

2. ***Inflation and Rising Costs***: Inflation erodes purchasing power over time, leading to higher prices for goods and services and reducing the value of savings and investments. Rising costs of living, including housing, healthcare, education, and utilities, can strain household budgets and diminish disposable income.

3. ***Market Volatility and Investment Risk***: Market volatility, fluctuations in asset prices, and investment risk can affect the value of investment portfolios, retirement savings, and long-term financial goals. Economic uncertainty and geopolitical events can contribute to market instability and create challenges for investors seeking to preserve and grow their wealth.

4. ***Debt Burden and Financial Stress***: High levels of debt, including credit card debt, student loans, mortgages, and personal loans, can increase financial stress and limit financial flexibility during economic downturns. Debt repayment obligations, interest payments, and debt service costs can strain household budgets and hinder progress toward financial goals.

5. ***Healthcare Costs and Insurance Coverage***: Rising healthcare costs, inadequate insurance coverage, and unexpected medical expenses can pose significant financial challenges for individuals and families. Healthcare expenses, including medical bills, prescription drugs, and health insurance premiums, can create financial hardship and disrupt financial planning efforts.

Strategies for Financial Resilience

To navigate economic challenges effectively and enhance financial resilience, individuals and families can implement various strategies to protect their financial well-being and mitigate risks:

1. ***Emergency Fund***: Build an emergency fund to cover unexpected expenses, such as job loss, medical emergencies, or car repairs. Aim to save three to six months' worth of living expenses in a liquid savings account or high-yield savings account to provide a financial safety net during times of crisis.

2. ***Budgeting and Expense Management***: Create a budget to track income and expenses, identify areas for saving or cutting back, and prioritize

essential expenses. Practice frugal living, avoid unnecessary expenses, and live within your means to maintain financial stability and build savings over time.

3. ***Diversified Income Streams***: Diversify sources of income by pursuing multiple streams of income, such as a side hustle, freelance work, rental income, or investment dividends. Diversified income streams provide resilience against job loss, income volatility, and economic downturns, reducing reliance on a single source of income.

4. ***Debt Management***: Manage debt responsibly by paying down high-interest debt, such as credit card debt, student loans, or personal loans, and avoiding excessive borrowing. Prioritize debt repayment, negotiate lower interest rates or payment plans, and explore debt consolidation or refinancing options to reduce financial burden and interest costs.

5. ***Risk Management and Insurance***: Protect against unforeseen risks and losses by maintaining adequate insurance coverage, including health insurance, life insurance, disability insurance, and property and casualty insurance. Review insurance policies regularly, understand coverage limits and exclusions, and adjust coverage as needed to mitigate financial risks.

6. ***Investment Strategy***: Develop a diversified investment strategy tailored to your risk tolerance, financial goals, and time horizon. Allocate assets across different asset classes, such as stocks, bonds, real estate, and alternative investments, to spread risk and minimize exposure to market volatility. Focus on long-term investing principles, such as dollar-cost averaging, asset allocation, and periodic rebalancing, to achieve consistent returns and build wealth over time.

7. ***Financial Education and Planning***: Invest in financial education and seek professional advice from certified financial planners, advisors, or wealth managers to develop a comprehensive financial plan. Set clear financial goals, establish a savings and investment strategy, and regularly review and adjust your plan based on changes in your financial situation, market conditions, and economic outlook.

8. ***Lifestyle Adjustments***: Make lifestyle adjustments and prioritize needs over wants to adapt to changing economic conditions and financial constraints. Cut discretionary expenses, negotiate lower rates or discounts, and explore cost-saving strategies to reduce spending without sacrificing quality of life. Focus on essential expenses, such as housing, food, healthcare, and education, and look for opportunities to optimize

spending and increase savings.

9. ***Community Support and Resources***: Seek support from family, friends, community organizations, and government agencies during times of financial hardship or crisis. Explore available resources, such as unemployment benefits, food assistance programs, housing assistance, and financial counseling services, to access support and guidance to navigate economic challenges effectively.

Learnings

Navigating economic challenges requires resilience, adaptability, and proactive financial planning to safeguard against potential risks and build long-term financial stability. By implementing strategies such as building an emergency fund, budgeting and expense management, diversified income streams, debt management, risk management and insurance, investment strategy, financial education and planning, lifestyle adjustments, and community support and resources, individuals and families can enhance their financial resilience and weather economic storms effectively.

Despite the uncertainties and challenges posed by economic downturns, inflation, market volatility, and other factors, individuals and families can take proactive steps to protect their financial well-being, mitigate risks, and achieve their long-term financial goals. Embrace the principles of financial resilience, adaptability, and preparedness to navigate economic challenges successfully and build a brighter financial future for yourself and your loved ones.

CHAPTER SEVENTEEN

Mindfulness and Money: Cultivating a Balanced Life Amidst Financial Goals

In the pursuit of financial success and security, it's easy to become consumed by goals, budgets, and investment strategies. However, amidst the hustle and bustle of managing finances, it's essential not to lose sight of the present moment and the importance of balance and well-being. Mindfulness, the practice of being fully present and aware of one's thoughts, feelings, and surroundings, can play a valuable role in achieving financial goals while fostering a sense of peace, contentment, and fulfillment in life. In this chapter, we'll explore the intersection of mindfulness and money, the benefits it offers, and strategies for cultivating a balanced life amidst financial goals.

Understanding Mindfulness and Money

Mindfulness is the practice of intentionally focusing one's attention on the present moment, without judgment or attachment to thoughts or emotions. It involves cultivating awareness, acceptance, and compassion for oneself and others, fostering a sense of clarity, calmness, and inner peace. Mindfulness can be applied to various aspects of life, including personal relationships, work, health, and finances, to promote well-being and reduce stress.

When it comes to money, mindfulness involves bringing awareness and intentionality to financial decisions, behaviors, and attitudes. It entails being conscious of one's spending habits, saving patterns, and investment choices, as well as understanding the emotional and psychological factors that influence financial behavior. By practicing mindfulness, individuals can develop a healthier relationship with money, cultivate financial well-being, and align their financial goals with their values and priorities.

Benefits of Mindfulness and Money

Mindfulness and money offer several benefits for individuals seeking to achieve financial goals while maintaining balance and well-being:

1. *Increased Awareness*: Mindfulness cultivates awareness of one's financial habits, patterns, and behaviors, allowing individuals to recognize and understand their relationship with money more deeply. By paying attention to spending triggers, emotional responses to money, and underlying beliefs about wealth and abundance, individuals can make more conscious and intentional financial decisions.
2. *Reduced Stress and Anxiety*: Mindfulness helps reduce stress, anxiety, and worry associated with money by promoting relaxation, acceptance, and equanimity. By practicing mindfulness techniques such as deep breathing, meditation, and visualization, individuals can manage financial stress more effectively, stay calm in challenging situations, and make clearer decisions about money.
3. *Improved Decision-Making*: Mindfulness enhances cognitive function and decision-making by promoting mental clarity, focus, and perspective. By approaching financial decisions with a clear mind and an open heart, individuals can evaluate options more objectively, weigh risks and benefits more effectively, and make choices that align with their long-term financial goals and values.
4. *Enhanced Financial Well-Being*: Mindfulness promotes a sense of financial well-being by fostering gratitude, contentment, and satisfaction with one's financial situation, regardless of external circumstances. By cultivating a mindset of abundance, generosity, and gratitude, individuals can experience greater fulfillment and joy in life, independent of their material wealth or possessions.
5. *Improved Relationships*: Mindfulness strengthens relationships by promoting empathy, compassion, and connection with oneself and others. By practicing mindful communication, active listening, and non-judgmental awareness, individuals can improve communication with

partners, family members, and friends about money, reducing conflicts and promoting mutual understanding and support.

Strategies for Cultivating Mindfulness and Money

To cultivate mindfulness and money in daily life, individuals can implement various strategies and practices:

1. *Mindful Spending*: Practice mindful spending by pausing before making purchases, reflecting on the true value and necessity of the item, and considering the long-term impact on your financial goals and well-being. Ask yourself whether the purchase aligns with your values and priorities, brings genuine joy or satisfaction, and contributes to your overall sense of fulfillment.

2. *Gratitude Practice*: Cultivate gratitude for the abundance and blessings in your life, including your financial resources, opportunities, and achievements. Practice gratitude rituals such as keeping a gratitude journal, expressing appreciation for what you have, and acknowledging the generosity of others. By focusing on gratitude, individuals can shift their perspective from scarcity to abundance and cultivate a sense of contentment and fulfillment.

3. *Financial Mindfulness Exercises*: Incorporate mindfulness exercises into your financial routine, such as mindful budgeting, mindful saving, and mindful investing. Set aside dedicated time to review your financial goals, track expenses, and monitor progress toward your objectives. Practice mindful breathing or meditation before making important financial decisions to cultivate clarity and focus.

4. *Self-Compassion and Acceptance*: Practice self-compassion and acceptance towards your self and your financial circumstances, recognizing that financial challenges and setbacks are a natural part of life. Be kind to yourself when facing financial difficulties, mistakes, or setbacks, and treat yourself with the same compassion and understanding you would offer to a friend in a similar situation.

5. *Intentional Consumption*: Practice intentional consumption by being mindful of your consumption habits, needs, and desires. Pause and reflect before making impulse purchases or succumbing to societal pressures to keep up with the Joneses. Consider whether your purchases

align with your values, contribute to your well-being, and support your long-term goals and priorities.

6. ***Mindful Investing***: Approach investing with mindfulness by focusing on the long-term perspective, rather than short-term fluctuations or market noise. Set clear investment goals, establish a diversified portfolio aligned with your risk tolerance and time horizon, and avoid emotional reactions to market volatility or media hype. Practice patience, discipline, and non-attachment to outcomes when it comes to investing, trusting in the power of compounding and staying committed to your investment strategy over time.

Learnings

Mindfulness and money offer a powerful combination for achieving financial goals while fostering balance, well-being, and fulfillment in life. By cultivating awareness, intentionality, and compassion in our financial decisions and behaviors, individuals can navigate the complexities of money with greater ease and clarity, reducing stress and promoting financial well-being.

Whether through mindful spending, gratitude practice, financial mindfulness exercises, self-compassion, intentional consumption, or mindful investing, there are various ways to incorporate mindfulness into our relationship with money and cultivate a more balanced and harmonious approach to financial management. Embrace the practice of mindfulness and money to create a more fulfilling and meaningful life, grounded in awareness, gratitude, and abundance.

CHAPTER EIGHTEEN

Conclusion: Empowering Yourself for Financial Success

Congratulations on completing this journey towards financial empowerment! Throughout this book, we've explored a wide range of topics, from understanding the basics of personal finance to delving into advanced investment strategies. Now, as we reach the conclusion, it's time to reflect on the key lessons learned and chart a course for achieving financial success and fulfillment in your life.

Reflecting on Your Financial Journey

Take a moment to reflect on your financial journey thus far. Consider the progress you've made, the challenges you've overcome, and the lessons you've learned along the way. Whether you're just starting out on your financial journey or you've been actively managing your finances for years, remember that every step you take towards financial empowerment brings you closer to your goals.

Key Takeaways

As you reflect on the chapters of this book, here are some key takeaways to keep in mind:

1. *Understanding Financial Basics*: Establish a solid foundation in financial literacy by understanding key concepts such as budgeting, saving, debt management, and investing. Take control of your finances by creating a budget, building an emergency fund, and managing debt responsibly.

2. ***Setting Financial Goals***: Define your financial goals and aspirations, both short-term and long-term. Whether it's buying a home, saving for retirement, or starting a business, clarity on your financial goals provides direction and motivation for your financial journey.

3. ***Investing for the Future***: Embrace the power of investing to grow your wealth and achieve financial independence. Develop an investment strategy tailored to your risk tolerance, time horizon, and financial objectives, and focus on diversification, long-term growth, and disciplined investing principles.

4. ***Embracing Frugality and Mindfulness***: Cultivate a mindset of frugality and mindfulness in your financial decisions and behaviors. Practice mindful spending, intentional consumption, and gratitude to align your financial choices with your values and priorities, fostering a sense of contentment and fulfillment in life.

5. ***Building Financial Resilience***: Prepare for economic challenges and uncertainties by building financial resilience. Establish an emergency fund, diversify income streams, manage debt responsibly, and maintain adequate insurance coverage to protect against unforeseen risks and disruptions.

6. ***Empowering Yourself***: Take ownership of your financial future and empower yourself to make informed decisions about money. Educate yourself, seek guidance from trusted advisors, and take action towards achieving your financial goals, one step at a time.

Charting Your Path Forward

Now that you've gained knowledge and insights into various aspects of personal finance and investing, it's time to chart your path forward towards financial success. Here are some steps to help you get started:

1. ***Review Your Financial Plan***: Review and update your financial plan based on the insights and strategies discussed in this book. Assess your current financial situation, set clear goals, and develop a roadmap for achieving them over time.

2. ***Take Action***: Take concrete steps towards implementing your financial plan and achieving your goals. Whether it's automating your savings, increasing your investment contributions, or paying down debt, take

action consistently to move closer to your objectives.

3. *Monitor Your Progress*: Regularly monitor your progress towards your financial goals and make adjustments as needed. Track your income, expenses, savings, and investment performance, and evaluate whether you're on track to meet your objectives.

4. *Continue Learning*: Stay curious and committed to lifelong learning in the field of personal finance and investing. Stay informed about market trends, financial products, and economic developments, and seek opportunities to expand your knowledge and skills.

5. *Celebrate Your Achievements*: Celebrate your achievements and milestones along the way, no matter how small. Recognize the progress you've made, the challenges you've overcome, and the lessons you've learned, and use these experiences to fuel your motivation and determination for the journey ahead.

Learnings

As you embark on your journey towards financial success, remember that it's not just about the destination but also the journey itself. Embrace the opportunities and challenges that come your way, and view them as valuable lessons and experiences that contribute to your growth and development.

By empowering yourself with knowledge, skills, and confidence, you have the ability to create a brighter financial future for yourself and your loved ones. Take ownership of your financial destiny, embrace the principles of financial empowerment, and chart a course towards a life of abundance, fulfillment, and prosperity.

Thank you for joining me on this journey towards financial empowerment. I wish you all the best on your path to financial success and fulfillment. Remember, the power to achieve your dreams lies within you. Empower yourself, take action, and make your financial aspirations a reality.